Chip Tricks

Chip Tricks

Look Like a Poker Pro

Ross Watson and Jen Teti

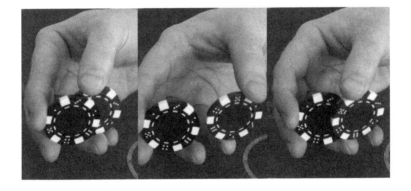

LYLE STUART
Kensington Publishing Corp.
www.kensingtonbooks.com

LYLE STUART BOOKS are published by

Kensington Publishing Corp.
850 Third Avenue
New York, NY 10022

Cover art and interior photographs by Heath Aiken (www.LaRoyStudios.com).

All Kensington titles, imprints, and distributed lines are available at special quantity discounts for bulk purchases for sales promotions, premiums, fund-raising, educational, or institutional use. Special book excerpts or customized printings can also be created to fit specific needs. For details, write or phone the office of the Kensington special sales manager: Kensington Publishing Corp., 850 Third Avenue, New York, NY 10022, attn: Special Sales Department; phone 1-800-221-2647.

Lyle Stuart is a trademark of Kensington Publishing Corp.

First printing: August 2006

10 9 8 7 6 5 4 3 2 1

Printed in the United States of America

ISBN 0-8184-0716-6

Contents

How'd They Do That?!

If you're reading this book, chances are good that you've already seen some chip tricks. Maybe you've seen them in person. If not, you've definitely witnessed a few if you've watched any poker on TV—and God knows it's hard not to have watched at least some poker on TV recently. It seems as if it's on every channel! The better-known players are even starting to become household names, some of the very same pros who make chip tricks look so easy! If you watched the 2004 World Series of Poker (WSOP) Tournament of Champions, you saw Annie Duke effortlessly and endlessly shuffling her chips on the way to the title. And during the 2003 WSOP, Antonio Esfandiari and Evelyn Ng made jaws drop with their finger feats. Watching these players is what inspired us to learn chip tricks.

Unfortunately, it wasn't that easy (and we're not even talking about actually learning the tricks); there were very few places to turn for good, complete information on how to perform chip tricks and *no books* that covered the material. That's why, after we mastered the tricks, we decided to write a book with detailed instructions and step-by-step pictures. This is that book.

Inside, you'll find that we break down all the top tricks for you. The most amazing thing is that after you practice for a while, you'll realize most of the tricks aren't very complicated. Well, okay, some of them are hard to master, but mostly they only appear difficult because they happen so quickly. This book solves that problem. Just read the instructions and look closely at the pictures, and you will never again wonder where your fingers need to go. It's that simple.

Chip Tricks

Look Like a Poker Pro

First Things First

We know you want to get started right away and we want that too, but there's something we need to tell you first. So sit tight, fondle your chips, and read the next part very carefully. It's important.

LEARN THE ALPHABET!

The tricks we've described in the section titled "The ABCs" are not only the easiest tricks to learn, they are also the most important, the very foundation for the more difficult tricks discussed later in the book.

If you practice and truly master them, you will not regret it, and you will soon notice that you learn harder tricks, like the Twirl, faster and easier than you learned some of the basic tricks. Amazing? Not really. All the time you put into learning the fundamentals will have resulted in *muscle* or *motor memory*. You may also have heard this called *kinesthetic memory* or *neuromuscular facilitation*. Whatever term is used, the result is the same: your fingers just seem to know what to do!

If you're still determined to learn the Butterfly first (one of the hardest tricks, if not the absolute hardest), we'll beg you one last time, don't! Our instructions are good—no, they're great—but they won't help. Would you try to do calculus without learning how to add and subtract first? Of course not, that's ridiculous; no textbook in the world could help you. You must learn the basics; there's no way around it. And you must practice.

PRACTICE MAKES PERFECT

We assume you have chips—now start carrying them around with you. Practice while you're playing poker online. (No one will see you drop the chips, although beware, they make an annoyingly harsh sound when bouncing off the keyboard!) Practice when you're watching TV, or when you're on the train. You can even practice while on the phone. After all, you only need one hand!

One amazing thing we've found is how quickly others will acclimate to your incessant practice habits. We both practiced in the office and found our work colleagues more than accommodating; in fact, nearly everyone we worked with eventually retrieved a chip of ours off the floor and handed it back—like a pencil. And both of our spouses got used to finding the occasional chip under the covers and neither one mentioned it. (Okay, that's a huge lie, but they didn't divorce us!)

Be sure to remember your manners when you're practicing outside of the house, though. Dropping a chip on a carpet is almost never a big deal, but dropping a chip and having to chase it down a movie theater aisle is significantly more problematic (trust us). Also, be conscious of the noise a particular trick makes. If you need to be close to silent, practice the knuckle roll. It's the quietest of the tricks . . . well, if you can actually do it without dropping the chip!

And, be sure to practice the tricks with both hands, not just your dominant hand. Give both hands a workout. You won't be sorry. It's not only more impressive to be able to do the tricks with both hands, but it also has synergistic qualities. You'll see: it won't take you nearly as long to learn the trick with the other hand as it did to learn the trick with your original hand! Plus, just imagine the applause when you're knuckle rolling with both hands simultaneously. You may need to stop and take a bow!

Truthfully, the basic tricks won't take you long to learn. You'll be doing them smoothly within a month. Don't misunderstand, they're not a cinch; you'll drop a lot of chips on the road to competence. Just keep at it. Also, get ready, you're about to field a lot of questions.

GET YOUR STORY STRAIGHT

"What are you doing with those chips?"

"You're learning to do what?! Why?!"

Although we've found most people to be extremely accommodating, it's only natural that when they first see you walking around with chips in your hands, they're going to ask you what's going on. Be ready with an answer.

You may have your own reasons, but here are some replies we suggest:

1. *Table cred.* If you're like us, you love poker, but you're light years from having anything that resembles an "A" game. Unfortunately, there's no substitute for the thousands of hours it's going to take to hone your skills; however, there are a variety of things you can do to appear to be a better poker player than you are. Perhaps the easiest thing is to learn a few chip tricks.

   We started with the thought that if we incorporated chip tricks into our game, we'd at least *look* like we knew what we were doing and . . . we were right. It did help. Believe it: if people see you easily flipping, flicking, and twisting chips, they'll think you've spent some time around the table and, consequently, may think twice before calling your bluff on the river. Chip tricks are respect magnets. Okay, they're low-powered refrigerator magnets, but they do earn you a little table credibility. They say, "Hey, I know what I'm doing—are you sure you want to test me?"

   Now, if you're a truly good player and you don't need chip tricks to buy you some time to figure out the difference between the flop and the river, knowing a few chip tricks is still worth your while; they get you instantly recognized as someone who knows the game. You don't have to wait to earn the respect you deserve.

We talk more about all this in a section later in the book entitled, "Table Smartz (Don't Look Like Dead Money)."

2. *Zen-like calm.* Gambling can be stressful, full of highs and lows. Repetitive motion is soothing. It can help you enter a semi-meditative state where you are less likely to lose your cool and overreact—even after a bad beat.

Anyone can understand that. Staying calm and collected in the face of adversity is universally acknowledged to be a good thing.

3. *Cards can be monotonous.* Unless you're very lucky or very willing to lose, playing good poker involves folding. A lot of folding. After folding your twelfth hand in a row, you may need the chip tricks to stay awake.

4. *Lookin' good in the 'hood.* Chip tricks are an accessory. Some people wear sunglasses and tacky shirts; others carry "lucky" trinkets with them to the table. Greg Raymer, the 2004 WSOP Main Event winner, brings fossils and wears lizard eye hologram sunglasses (don't make fun, he's a millionaire). You can bring your chip tricks.

5. *The "wow" factor.* Your friends will be amazed. Amazed by the tricks or possibly amazed that they're *your* friends. It could go either way.

6. *Confidence.* Thomas Carlyle once said, "Nothing builds self-esteem and self-confidence like accomplishment."

No truer words were ever spoken. You can't imagine how good you'll feel about yourself after mastering just one or two of the tricks. Silly? Maybe. True? Undoubtedly. Enjoy it!

Meet the Chips

You're ready to get started, you're raring to go. Great. Here are a few easy exercises you can do to warm up and start to develop a feel for the chips.

Keep in mind that these are exercises, not tricks. They are simple, so you shouldn't have to practice very long to master what we're going to discuss next.

Before we begin, though, we must issue a caveat regarding the names of the exercises/tricks listed in this book: many of them are commonly known by one name but sometimes by another. We title them with the best-known name and list any alternate names under "aka."

Also, please note that all the instructions were written from a right-handed perspective, and the pictures are of us performing the tricks right-handed. We have nothing against lefties and we encourage you to learn the tricks with both hands, but we're playing the odds here; most people are right-handed.

Now, let's get started!

THE RESTACK (aka: Pullover)

This exercise is almost insultingly easy, and it definitely doesn't qualify as a trick, but it's worth practicing for a few reasons:

1. *Develop great touch/feel.* Feel it! That's what this exercise is all about. We're trying to develop your touch, and the

only way to do that is to have you lift a lot of chips and become familiar with their weight and their feel.

Plus, considering that the weight and feel of chips often varies from one location to another (we'll get into this more in the appendix entitled "The Lowdown on Poker Chips"), it's a good habit to do the restack a few times whenever you first sit down anywhere because the restack is safe. There's no way you're going to drop chips on the floor, bounce one into your eye (or worse, someone else's), or have one roll across the table when all you're trying to do is the restack. Therefore, it allows you to acquaint yourself with the new chips with absolutely no risk.

2. *It actually looks cool.* It does. Seriously. If you do it fast enough, it can make you look mechanical. *Watch out, you're a poker machine!*

3. *It's the prerequisite for the shuffle.* If you intend to learn the shuffle—and chances are, if you bought this book, you probably do—you need to know how to do the restack. It's what allows you to shuffle continuously.

Getting Started

For the restack, you need 2–8 chips. We think it looks best with 4–8, but you can go through some hard times at the table and may find yourself with as few as 2 measly chips. This trick will work for you even then.

Let's begin with 6.

Step One. Place the chips in a single stack.

Step Two. Place your hand over the stack. Think of a clock: Your thumb is at 9 o'clock, and your fingers fan between 11 o'clock and 5 o'clock. Here are two pictures showing the grip from different angles. This grip is very important. We want you to get it.

Step Three. Pick up half of the stack and move it to the outside (the side that the majority of your fingers are on).

Step Four. Reach back with your thumb and index finger, and pick up the remaining chips.

Step Five. Place that stack on top of the stack that you moved first.

Before You Move On

Make sure you can do the restack quickly! And if you haven't noticed, the restack travels across the table when you do it multiple times, so unless you have a lot of room, you'll need to slide the final stack back to a more central position before doing it again.

THE CHATTER STACK

This exercise also will help you develop your touch and will come in handy when you're learning the shuffle.

Getting Started

You can do this with any number of chips, but for our purposes, just grab the same 6 you used for the restack.

Step One. Place the chips in a single stack and then place your hand over the stack. The finger positioning is the same as for the restack.

Step Two. Use your fingers to lift the entire stack off of the table slightly (no more than ½ inch), then lift your hand up and drop the chips—one after another, starting with the bottom chip—back down onto the table, reforming the original stack.

This exercise has only two steps because it really is just that easy!

Before You Move On

Practice dropping the chips both slowly and quickly. Concentrate on your rhythm. Listen to the chips and try to drop each one at the same pace. And don't let the chatter drive you crazy!

THE SPIN

This one's harder. In fact, it's much harder, so don't be discouraged if you don't master it instantly. And don't worry, your practice won't go to waste; the spin is actually a very important component of both Twirls taught in this book.

Getting Started

You only need one chip for this exercise.

Step One. Hold the chip between your ring and index fingers. It needs to be gripped somewhere between your first knuckle and the tip of both fingers. Do what's comfortable, but remember that the closer you hold it to the tips of your fingers, the easier the chip will spin out of your grip.

If your hand is too small to do this comfortably, hold the chip between your index and pinky fingers.

Step Two. Put your middle finger on the outside edge of the chip and use it to spin the chip clockwise 180 degrees by pulling it back toward the palm of your hand.

The problem most people experience when they are trying to learn the spin is that the chip starts to travel, meaning, it moves during the rotation. Generally, the bottom of the chip starts to edge toward the tip of the ring finger (or pinky, depending on the grip you use). If the chip is moving for you, try this: imagine a rod between your ring and index fingers. Then try to rotate the chip, using this imaginary rod as the axis. Sometimes a little visualization can go a long way!

Step Three. Move your middle finger back behind the outside edge of the chip. Now you're ready to spin again!

Before You Move On

You really don't want the chip to be moving very much during the spin. The way you can test this is to see if you can do the spin several times in a row without needing to reset the chip. If you can spin it several times in a row, you've probably mastered this exercise. If you can't, and the imaginary axis isn't helping, you need to find a different way to work on stabilizing the chip. Try experimenting with different grip tensions; it may be that you're just not holding the chip tightly enough between your index and ring (or pinky) fingers.

THE REBOUND

We'll end the warm-up exercises with a fun one.

Getting Started

You need one chip for this exercise and an appropriate surface on which to rebound the chip. A regulation poker table is ideal, but anything soft yet firm will work.

Step One. Hold the chip between your thumb and index or middle finger; which finger you use is a matter of personal preference. You can successfully perform this exercise gripping the chip either way. Here we're holding it between thumb and index finger.

Step Two. While holding the chip vertically, release or forcefully bounce the chip onto the table/surface. On a springy surface, you can practically just drop the chip. A harder surface will require you to bounce the chip with some force.

Step Three. Catch the chip after the bounce but before it hits the surface. This actually requires a certain amount of coordination and catlike quickness, and might just remind you of a game of jacks!

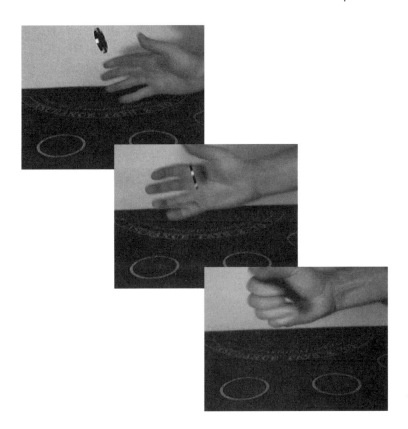

Before You Move On

The height the chip will rebound is determined by both the surface and the force with which the chip is dropped or bounced. Practice dropping or bouncing at different speeds, and note the height of the resulting rebound.

Also, practice releasing the chip at different angles, and take note of the direction of the resulting bounce. You will need this information in order to successfully master the Bounce, which is detailed later in this book.

The ABCs

You've made it! You're about to learn some actual tricks. Woohoo! At the risk of annoying you, we'll say it one more time: please don't jump ahead. Just as you worked your way through the chip exercises before getting to the ABCs, now work your way through the ABCs before going on to the harder tricks. These are the basic tricks; it's in your best interest to truly master them before attempting harder stuff.

THE FRONT TO BACK *(aka: Thumb Roll, Thumb Flip, or Thumb Chip Flip)*

Okay, first, a rant: The fact that this trick is commonly known as the Front to Back is ridiculous. "Front to back" describes many tricks! That's why we personally avoid calling this trick the Front to Back. Instead, we call this trick the Thumb Roll. It's catchy, it's a fun play on words—and it actually describes the trick. You roll the chip up and over with your thumb! Therefore, that's how we're going to refer to it here. The Thumb Roll! Just know that we are currently the only two people on the planet who refer to it this way. Hopefully, you'll join the Thumb Roll revolution!

Anyway, name controversy aside; we consider the, ahem, Thumb Roll to be the single most important chip trick. That's why we're teaching it first. It's the foundation for many other tricks. To mention only a few, the Thumb Roll sets up the vertical switches, the classic Twirl and—thumb roll, er, drum roll, please . . . the Butterfly. Are you ready?

Getting Started

The Thumb Roll requires a minimum of 2 chips, but it's actually easier to learn with more chips in your hand. The maximum number of chips you can use will depend solely on the size of your hand. Most people can manage 5 or 6 with no problem.

Grab 4 to start.

Step One. Stand the chips straight up between your index, middle, and ring fingers. The pinky sits this trick out.

The chips need to be fairly stable for this trick. You will know you have the right grip pressure if you are able to turn your hand upside down without dropping the chips.

Step Two. Use your thumb to loosen the outer chip. Just gently roll it up a bit.

Step Three. Continue to use your thumb to roll the chip up the index finger. The chip will naturally start to fall across the other chips.

Step Four. Use your thumb to guide the chip over and down.

If you're having trouble with this trick, it's probably because it's hard for you to keep the inner chips stable during the flip. One thing you can do to combat this is angle your hand down during the trick.

Before You Move On

Make sure that your thumb is truly guiding the chip through the entire trick. If the chip feels out of control on the way over and down, even just a little, you need to keep practicing.

Also, try to do the Thumb Roll with only 2 chips. This is the hardest version of the trick because you don't have the weight of the additional inner chips to help with the stabilization. If you can do the Thumb Roll with only 2 chips, you have the trick down.

Just for Fun

See if you can roll 2 or even 3 chips over the top. Once you're good, you'll find it easy!

THE FINGER CHIP FLIP *(aka: Finger Flip, Index Chip Flip, or just Index Flip)*

We have a special place in our heart for the Finger Chip Flip: it's the first real trick we learned! It's also a classic, so pay attention!

Getting Started

The finger chip flip requires at least 2 chips. You can do it with 4, 5, or 6, but let's start with 3. When you can perform the 3-chip variation with ease, you'll be able to transition up or down in chip number with no problems, guaranteed.

Step One. Hold the 3 chips with your thumb and index finger. Make sure your thumb and index finger are slightly above the midpoint of the chips.

Step Two. This is the most difficult step of the trick. Use your ring finger to roll the two inner chips down. At the same time, use your index finger to roll the outer chip up ever so slightly; you probably won't even have to work on this part: it happens naturally as you roll the two inner chips down. Note that your pinky and middle fingers are not involved in this step and shouldn't be touching the chips.

Step Three. Now pull the uppermost chip down (back toward the palm of your hand) with your index finger. The outer chip should flip over the inner chips. Your middle finger provides stability for the outer chip during the flip, functioning as a rail.

Step Four. Your index finger guides the chip through the entire flip.

As the outer chip flips over the inner chips, make sure your index finger is applying sufficient pressure to keep the flipped chip firmly pressed against the chips in front of it. The flipped chip will continue to fall down behind the chips in front of it and will be

snugly caught by the thumb and ring finger. Once perfected, all aspects of this final step will seem to occur simultaneously.

Before You Move On

Just like the Thumb Roll, see if you can do this trick with only 2 chips. Extra chips add stability. Make sure you can do without that crutch.

Just for Fun

Test yourself: See how many Finger Chip Flips you can do in 10 seconds, then try to beat it. Admittedly, at times it's hard to push yourself to continue practicing; this is a great technique to keep your motivation level high, especially after you think you've mastered a trick. Remember, additional speed will almost always enhance the look of a trick; even simple tricks look spectacular when done super fast.

THE SWITCHES

The name is an apt description: these tricks involve switching a chip from the front of a stack to the back or from the back of a stack to the front.

This group of lesser-known tricks, the Switches, look deceptively easy. Their simplicity in appearance and economy of movement make them ideal table tricks, but as you're about to learn, one shouldn't confuse this appearance with a low level of difficulty.

Vertical Front-to-Back Switch (Kick-Out Method)

The Vertical Front-to-Back Switch can be done a couple of ways; however, learning the kick-out method first will most likely enable you to master this trick more quickly than if you started with the classic method, which we'll describe after the kick-out. Once you've learned both ways to do the trick, you'll probably favor the classic method, as it both looks and feels much smoother, but in order to get you switching the classic way, let's first jump into the kick-out method.

Getting started. We're going to use 2 chips to learn this trick, so grab 2 chips of different color. As with many of the tricks in this book, once you've got it down, you can pretty much add chips to the trick at will.

Step One. Hold the 2 chips between your ring and index fingers, slightly below the middle of the chip. If necessary, you can use your middle finger to keep the chips stable.

Step Two. Using your thumb, roll the outer chip up the index finger, angling the chip inward. You can get the chip to angle inward by rolling your thumb to the right a bit. If the top of the chip isn't angling inward toward your palm, you're probably rolling your thumb and chip vertically, thus creating no angle.

Step Three. While holding the outer chip with your thumb at its peak on the index finger, move your middle finger behind the lower chip.

Step Four. Using the backside tip of your middle finger, push the edge of the chip outward slightly. As you'll learn and feel, an ever so slight push outward is really all that is needed for the trick to be successful.

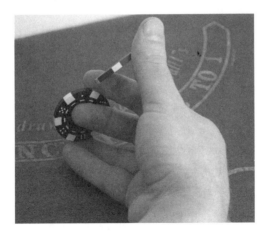

Step Five. Using your thumb, roll the top chip down behind the lower one. Step Four creates just enough space for the top chip to roll down with ease.

Before you move on. Make sure you can do this trick smoothly, especially Step Two. The more comfortable you are with rolling and angling the outer chip up your index finger with your thumb, the easier the Classic Switch will be to learn.

Just for fun. After you've got this down, try doing it with 4 chips. Switch 2 chips at the same time from the front to the back.

Vertical Front-to-Back Switch (Classic Method)

You're going to look like Joe Cool at the poker table once you've got this one down.

Getting started. As before, grab 2 chips, one of each color. Having chips of different color will help provide contrast, enabling others to see the movement of your tricks more clearly.

Step One. This step is the same as in the kick-out method.

Step Two. As in the kick-out method, using your thumb, roll the outer chip up the index finger angling the chip inward (toward your palm). Now comes the big difference: As you're rolling the

outer chip up the index finger, the index finger is going to roll the inner chip across the ring finger so that the inner chip is now touching both the ring finger and the pinky.

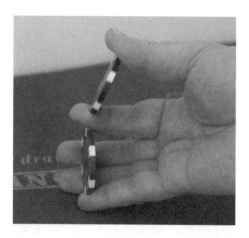

The rolling of the inner chip serves the same purpose as the kick-out served in the previous trick: it creates space. You'll see it in the next step.

Step Three. Straighten the top chip so that it is no longer at an angle. Do this by slightly pushing the chip outward with your thumb.

Step Four. Using your index finger, roll the bottom chip back across your ring finger, and at the same time, roll the top chip down with your thumb ever so slightly. The final position of the chips should be the same as the starting position, only with the inner and outer chips switched.

Before you move on. Quicken the speed of this trick. As with most of these tricks, the faster you can do it the smoother it looks. Keep practicing until you can do the trick so seamlessly that it looks like one step instead of four.

Just for fun. Try alternating between the kick-out and classic methods of the Vertical Front-to-Back Switch. It may look like the same trick to others, but you'll know it's actually two tricks. Enjoy your secret!

Vertical Back-to-Front Switch

Okay, you've got the Vertical Front-to-Back Switch down! Well, let's do it in reverse. Some tricks are more difficult for one person than another; this trick is one that tends to be hard to learn for most people. Don't think that just because you've mastered the Front-to-Back Switch that this similar trick is going to be a cinch to learn.

Getting started. Just like all the other switches, grab 2 chips of different colors to get started.

Step One. Hold the 2 chips between your ring and index fingers, slightly below the middle of the chip.

Step Two. Using your thumb, roll the inner chip up the index finger, angling the top of the chip inward slightly. While doing this, thrust out slightly with your ring finger; this will cause the outer chip to angle inward slightly too. You'll need to practice a lot and tweak this step along with Step Three before you'll be able to unveil it at the table.

Step Three. The slant at which you rolled the inner chip up your index finger combined with the slight inward lean of the outer chip should provide enough of an angle for you to roll the inner chip in front of the outer chip.

Before you move on. Again, this trick will take some serious practice before you're able to execute it consistently. Don't despair though; keep practicing: while this trick may not look flashy, few if any of your poker buddies will be able to show this one off.

Just for fun. After you can do this trick smoothly try incorporating the Spin exercise you learned. After rolling the back chip up, spin the front chip before switching the back chip to the front. If you can do this the Twirl is going to be a cinch for you to learn.

Horizontal Back-to-Front Switch

While the vertical switches involved rolling a chip up your index finger, the horizontal switches involve rolling a chip across your ring and pinky fingers, keeping the rolling chip parallel to the floor—hence the name "horizontal."

Getting started. As with all of the switches we'll be describing here, we suggest using 2 chips of different colors.

Step One. Similar to the vertical switches, position the 2 chips between your ring and index fingers, slightly below the middle of the chip. The middle finger can either be touching the chips or not. If you still need a picture for this step you may want to reconsider your interest in chip tricks.

Step Two. Position your thumb on the inner chip, slightly above your index finger. The exact place your thumb touches the inner chip will vary depending on the length of your fingers; however, it typically lines up at about the middle of the thumbnail.

Step Three. In a sweeping motion with your thumb, roll the inner chip across your ring to your pinky. The inner chip should be rolled entirely past the outer chip; this will ensure that you'll have enough room for the switch. The middle finger is not used in this trick; however, if you're having difficulty keeping the chip between your index and ring fingers stable you may want to keep the middle finger touching this chip as this tends to increase stability.

Step Four. As the inner chip rolls past the outer chip, slightly bend the fingers that are holding the outer chip—the index and ring fingers—inward. This bending movement will position what was previously the outer chip to the inner position. We've exaggerated the bend in this set of pictures so that you can see what we're talking about. It doesn't have to be this extreme to work.

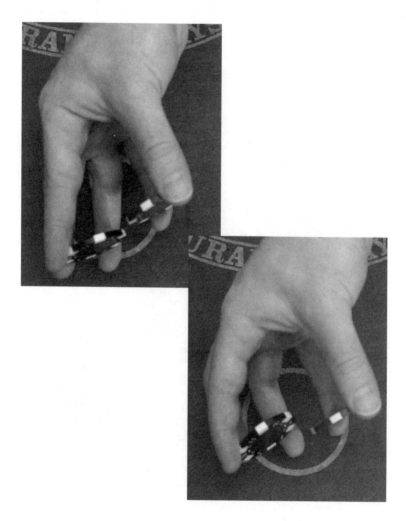

Step Five. Move the chip that is now innermost (the chip between your index and ring fingers) behind the outermost chip by moving your ring and index fingers toward your thumb and pinky until this chip is directly behind the outer chip. At this point all fingers other than the middle finger should be touching both chips (*all* fingers for those using the middle finger for stability). Reposition the fingers back into the starting position to do the trick again.

Your fingers are now positioned to do the trick again. All the switches look best when performed multiple times in a row.

Before you move on. Make sure you're moving the chip between your index and ring fingers smoothly behind the outer chip (Step Five). An incorrect Step Five can make the trick look sloppy and can make it very hard to reposition the fingers back into the starting position. If you're having difficulty during Step Five ensuring that the inner chip is entirely flush against the outer chip, use your middle finger to push the inner chip against the outer chip.

Just for fun. Figure out the maximum number of chips you can switch from the front to the back. Can you do 8 chips, switching 4 of them from the front to the back?

Horizontal Back-to-Front Flip

If you've mastered the Horizontal Back-to-Front Switch, the chip flip variety will be very easy to learn. If you don't have the non-flip variety down, keep practicing that one as this one will come with ease once you have the other in your repertoire.

Getting started. Steps One and Two are the same as the non-flip variety.

Step One. Position the two chips between your ring and index fingers, slightly below the middle of the chip, with your thumb positioned on the inner chip, almost touching your index finger.

Step Two. Using your thumb, roll the inner chip about two thirds of the way past the outer chip. The inner chip should be between your thumb and pinky at this point.

Step Three. Using your middle finger, push the outer edge of the outer chip inward. This action will cause the outer chip to flip around the inner chip. If the inner chip starts to rotate while you're pushing the outer chip, you either need to roll the inner chip farther past the outer chip or, more likely, you need to hold the inner chip more firmly between your thumb and pinky.

Step Four. Ensure that the flipped chip is flush against the outer chip by pushing the flipped chip in with your index finger. As you get better with this trick you'll have greater control of the flips and you'll only use this step now and then.

Before you move on. Make sure you've spent adequate time practicing the flip maneuver (Step Three). For this trick to look good you need to be able to do more than just flip the chip: you must be able to flip it smoothly so that it looks as though you have total control of the chip as it's flipping.

Just for fun. Try alternating between the non-flip and flip versions of this trick to spice things up a bit.

Horizontal Front-to-Back Switch

Similar to the Vertical Back-to-Front Switch, this trick is more difficult than it looks. The rolling and switching in these tricks can feel awkward; the chips just don't naturally want to go in the direction we're pushing them. Mastering both the Vertical Back-to-Front Switch and Horizontal Front-to-Back Switch will set you apart from the crowd.

Getting started. Grab 2 chips to get started.

Step One. Position the 2 chips between your ring and index fingers, slightly below the middle of the chip. You should be able to do this step in your sleep by now.

Step Two. Apply a lot of pressure to the inner chip with your ring and index fingers such that the inner chip is gripped very firmly and the outer chip much more loosely. Using your thumb, roll the outer chip onto your pinky. If you're having difficulty separating the outer chip from the inner chip when attempting this roll, you're probably either gripping the outer chip too firmly or you're not reaching over far enough with your thumb to roll the outer chip. The thumb should only be touching the outer chip when performing this roll. This is by far the most difficult step and will take much practice before it comes to you with ease.

Step Three. Shift the inner chip around the outer chip by extending and pushing the index and middle fingers outward, then bring those fingers back in toward the thumb and pinky. This movement will switch the position of the chips.

Before you move on. Take solace in that this is the last of the switches. Hopefully you haven't switched from enjoying chip tricks to being utterly frustrated with them. Just remember that all this practice will pay off in the end; this is kind of like learning to ride a bike: once you've got it you never lose it.

Just for fun. See if you can do all the switches one right after another.

THE PULL-UP

If your body type is anything like the stereotypical poker player, you should find this trick much easier than an actual pull-up!

Getting Started

Similar to the Finger Chip Flip, grab 3 chips to start.

Step One. Grip the chips at their midpoint between your thumb and middle finger. The ring and pinky fingers should not be touching the chips; they sit this trick out.

Step Two. Use your index finger to reach over the top of the chips and pull the front chip up.

If you're having problems getting the front chip to loosen, try getting your index finger as close to the bottom of the front chip as possible before starting to pull it up.

Step Three. When at least a quarter of the front chip is above the other two, use the pad of your index finger to grip the chip and carefully pull it back toward your palm. The chip will then naturally fall over the other two chips.

Step Four. Use the outside of your index finger to guide the front chip down. It is now the innermost chip.

Before You Move On

As with many other tricks, chip stability can be an issue in the Pull-Up. There will almost always be slight movement when you first start the Pull-Up, but for the most part, the inner chips should stay still and stand straight during this trick. If they don't, experiment with how high or low you grip the chips between your thumb and middle finger. The length of your fingers will dictate what will work best for you.

Just for Fun

Pull the front chip up, and try to balance it atop the other two chips in a "T" formation.

THE SOMERSAULT

Remember the Restack, the exercise we did at the beginning of the book? Well, here's a cool variation of it that definitely qualifies as a trick.

Getting Started

You need 3 chips.

Step One. It's the same as the Restack. Place the 3 chips in a single stack.

Step Two. Again, this is the same. Place your hand over the stack in the correct position.

Step Three. Almost the same . . . Pick up *2* chips and restack them on the outside.

Step Four. Place your index finger between the new stack and the original chip. Your index finger should be at about 1 o'clock on the original chip.

Using your thumb, lift the outer edge of the original chip up and somersault it over until it is resting atop the new stack. Use your index finger at first for leverage, but then get it out of the way.

Step Five. Allow momentum to carry the chip through its tumble toward settling atop the new stack.

For this to look right, the original chip should be touching the table until the very end.

Be aware that like the Restack, the Somersault travels. At some point, you will need to slide the stack back to where you originally started if you plan on doing this trick a number of times in succession.

Before You Move On

Make sure you can somersault the chip consistently atop the other 2 chips. It's not as easy as it looks. It you're having trouble and you just can't get it down, try this: don't take your thumb off the chip during the Somersault. Just let your thumb guide it the whole way. If you use your thumb as a guide, there's absolutely no way to blow this trick, and this method will allow you to get a better feel for how the chip needs to fall onto the stack. With a little practice, you may soon graduate to doing the trick without your thumb guiding the chip the entire way.

Just for Fun

Alternate the Somersault with the Restack. As always, try to do them fast!

THE CHIP SNAPS

These are aptly named tricks both because they make a snapping noise *and* they're a snap to learn. Their simplicity is hard to overstate: We've seen ten-year-olds master them quickly.

Bottom Chip Snap

Again, this is probably the easiest trick in the book, though it has many of the trappings found in more difficult tricks.

Getting started. Grab 2 chips, one of each color.

Step One. Hold these 2 chips flat between your thumb and index finger, positioning your thumb in the middle of the top chip with the bottom chip extending half a chip length to the left beyond the upper chip. Make sure you position your middle, ring, and pinky fingers above the chips. The easiest way to ensure that these fingers are positioned correctly when you're first learning this trick is to curl them into your hand.

Step Two. Forcefully bring your middle finger down (or uncurl it) on the extended edge of the bottom chip. This action will flip the bottom chip and will situate the bottom chip between your index and middle fingers.

Step Three. In one quick motion, pull your index finger out from between the 2 chips. It's important that pressure is applied to the top chip by the thumb while this is occurring. After you remove your index finger you'll hear a snapping noise made by the 2 chips smacking together.

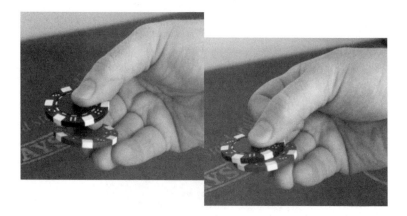

Step Four. Move the 2 chips from between the thumb and middle finger to between the thumb and index finger. This puts the chips back in the starting position so you can repeat the trick. Since the snapping noise is what gives this trick personality, it's best to repeat this trick many times.

Before you move on. Make sure you're getting a loud snapping noise from this trick. If this isn't happening for you, just apply more pressure with your thumb during Step Three as you're removing your index finger from between the chips.

Just for fun. You can increase the difficulty of this trick by alternating the fingers that flip the bottom chip. Start with your middle finger, then use your ring finger, then your pinky, and then back to your middle finger.

Top Chip Snap

Almost identical to the Bottom Chip Snap, though with your hand position flipped.

Getting started. Again, we'll use 2 chips, one of each color.

Step One. The easiest way to position the chips correctly is to start as you would for the Bottom Chip Snap, then rotate your hand 180 degrees (that would be a half turn for those of you who are mathematically impaired). At this point, your thumb should be underneath the middle of the bottom chip with the bottom chip extending half a chip length to the left beyond the upper chip. Your middle, ring, and pinky fingers should be below the chips.

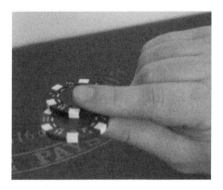

Step Two. With your middle finger, push the extended edge of the top chip up. This action will flip the top chip and situate it between your index and middle fingers.

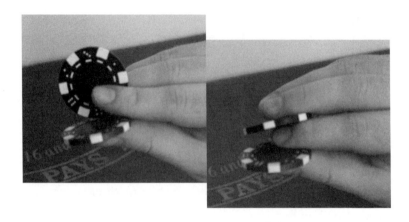

Step Three. As with the Bottom Chip Snap, pull your index finger out from between the two chips. It's important that pressure is applied to the top chip by your middle finger while this is occurring. After you remove your index finger you'll hear a snapping noise made by the two chips smacking together.

Step Four. This is the same as with the Bottom Chip Snap: move the two chips from between the thumb and middle fingers to between the thumb and index finger. This puts the chips back in the starting position so you can repeat the trick.

Before you move on. As with the Bottom Chip Snap, make sure you're consistently getting a loud snapping noise. If not, you'll need to apply more pressure to the middle finger in Step Three.

Just for fun. Another way to increase the difficulty of the Chip Snaps is to alternate between the Bottom Chip Snap and the Top Chip Snap.

The Spice of Life

If you've mastered the tricks taught in the previous section, congratulations! You now know a nice number of chip tricks and can probably already impress at the table. Well done.

Some of you may be thinking, "I know enough tricks; I don't need to learn more." To those people we say, "Great. We're glad you got what you wanted out of the book." Most of you, however, probably want to learn more tricks and that's exactly what this section's about—more.

In this section, we teach a wide range of tricks. Some are classics like the shuffle. Others are less useful (read: too risky to use at the table) but still fun to know how to do. Flip through this section and learn whatever appeals to you. The more tricks you learn, the more variety you will have in your chip trick arsenal. Not only is that a good way to look like a poker pro, but we've also heard it said that variety is the spice of life. Enjoy!

THE SHUFFLE *(aka: Riffle)*

This may be the most common chip trick in the universe. You see it everywhere, and almost everyone who has spent any time around a poker table has mastered it. You need to, too. It's not that hard.

Getting Started

This trick can be done with as few as 4 chips. The maximum number you can use, however, varies with individual hand size.

Save your maximum for later, though. To begin, grab 6 chips. Grab 3 of one color and 3 of another color; that way you can tell if you're really shuffling the chips or just shoving them together!

An ideal surface to practice this trick on is, obviously, a poker table, but again, anything soft yet firm will work. We've done it successfully on a hard pillow, a sofa, even a mouse pad. Stay away from slippery tables; they just won't work.

Step One. Use the Restack to create two 3-chip stacks. The stacks should touch each other.

Step Two. Place your hand around the stacks. Your thumb and index finger are stationed around the left stack in the 9 o'clock and 11 o'clock positions. Your middle finger is in the—well, middle; it touches both stacks. The rest of your fingers are fanned along the right side of the right stack.

Step Three. Lift the stacks up ever so slightly with your middle finger while raising your hand. With any luck, the chips will start to form one stack. Be gentle! This trick is not about strength; it's about touch.

Step Four. Use your thumb and pinky to push the stacks together until they form one 6-chip stack.

Step Five. Repeat. If you shuffle them correctly, the stacks will be back to their original stack coloring in 3 short shuffles! Cool, huh?

This is what the stack should look like after your second shuffle.

This is what the stack should look like after the third and final shuffle.

Ta-da!

Before You Move On

Try another starting position. Putting your middle finger between the two stacks is just one method of shuffling chips. It works best for us, but there's another starting position you should also test out. It may work better for you: Instead of your middle finger, put your index finger between the two stacks. In this starting position, your middle finger is positioned at two o'clock on the right chip stack. Now try shuffling a few times. Continue practicing using whatever method works best for you. Remember, the goal is consistent shuffling!

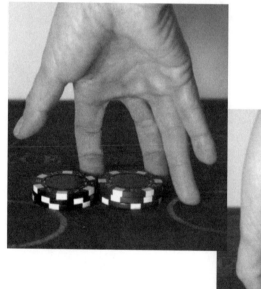

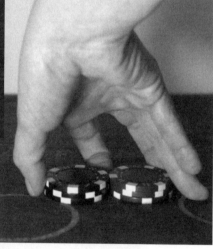

Just for Fun

Try to shuffle 4-chip stacks. If that's a piece of cake for you, try shuffling 5-chip stacks!

THE BOTTOM CHIP FLIP

This is an easy trick with an added bonus—it *looks* hard!

Getting Started

You can do this trick with as few as 3 chips, but it looks better with a bigger stack.

Grab 6 chips.

Step One. Place your hand over the stack of chips. Your thumb is at 7 o'clock and the rest of your fingers fan from 11 to 6 o'clock.

Step Two. Tilt the chips forward (away from your body), using your thumb to lift the chips.

Step Three. To be clear here, let's number the chips 1 to 6 from the top of the stack down. Use your fingers to slide all but the bottom chip (#6) toward the palm of your hand. Your middle and ring fingers will end up in the middle of that chip.

Here's what it looks like from the front.

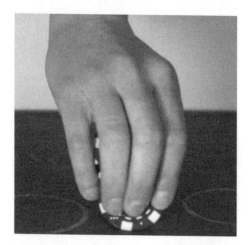

Step Four. Use your thumb to push the bottom chip forward. When your thumb comes into full contact with the bottom chip of the raised stack (#5), release the chip #6 onto the table.

Step Five. Use your thumb to pull chip #5 toward the palm of your hand. Then slide the chip up behind the raised stack. While sliding the chip up the side, allow the rest of the chips (#1–#4) to fall atop chip #6 on the table. Rest the chip you've been sliding up the side on the top of the stack: what started out as #5 is now #1. This seems like a lot to be doing, but it happens rather naturally.

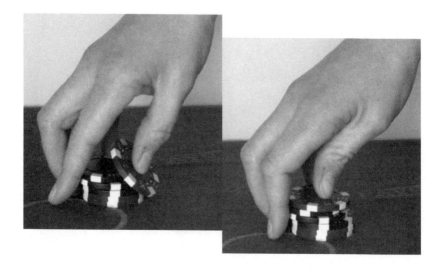

Before You Move On

As we said before, this looks better with a big stack. Make sure you can do this with at least 8 chips.

Just for Fun

Try it with both hands at the same time.

THE CHIP SWEEP

This can be an addictive trick because it's both easy to learn and impressive to watch. Your spouse and/or parents won't believe you when you tell them you're addicted to sweeping!

Getting Started

Grab 8 chips for this trick and hold them in a stack alternating chip colors. For this trick, you're going to need a surface that has a little give. Practice surfaces that have worked well for us have been a sofa, ottoman, and ironing board. Just imagine the conversation you'll have with your significant other: "Honey, I'll be downstairs practicing sweeping, and I'll have the ironing board tied up for a while as well." They won't know what got in to you!

Step One. This may actually be the most difficult part of the trick. We're sure you've seen the pros take a stack of chips and push it into the pot in such a way that the chips fan out perfectly. For our purposes, using your right hand, fan the chips to your left. This is actually much easier than it looks though it will take a bit of practice to consistently do this well. It's important that all chips, except the one to the extreme left, have a piece of the chip to their right underneath them.

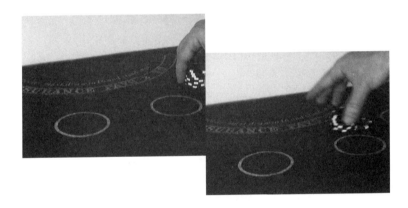

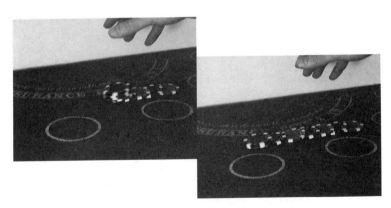

Step Two. Pick up the chip farthest to the left, holding it between your index finger and thumb. Ensuring that you're holding this chip correctly is essential to the success of this trick. Your thumb and index finger should be perpendicular to each other.

Step Three. In a quick yet soft movement, run the chip between your thumb and index finger from left to right, across all the chips. The pressure you're applying to the chips on the surface should be hard enough to hear the clicking of chips hitting each other yet soft enough not to disturb the fan.

Step Four. After running the chip between your thumb and index finger across the fan, lift up your thumb, allowing the chip to rest on both the index finger and the surface.

Step Five. Sweep the chips up into your hand. You'll discover whether or not the surface you're using is adequate during this step. The first chip swept won't easily slide on top of the chip on your index finger if the surface is too hard.

After all the chips have been swept into your hand, bring your thumb down on the last chip. This allows you to cleanly lift all the chips up from the surface.

Another thing to note about this step is that you need to do it quickly. It not only looks better, but it's also critical to the success of this step. Going too slowly can result in half success; you'll probably end by messing up the fan along the way.

Before You Move On

Practice Step One a lot. While this step depends heavily on the surface, it also depends on the little toss or push that you give to the chips, and because of this, consistency only develops after quite a bit of practice. If you just can't seem to get Step One down, you can always place the chips in a fan one chip at a time; however, doing this takes a lot of the flash from the trick.

Just for Fun

As we've previously mentioned, being able to perform tricks with both hands is pretty impressive. This is especially true of the Chip Sweep. Try sweeping back and forth, sweeping with your right hand, then your left. (To sweep with your left hand, just do everything the same as with your right hand but in the opposite direction.)

THE BOUNCE

Here's a trick where you bounce a chip from the felt onto the top of a stack of chips. While you already know that it's easy to bounce a chip, you will soon find out that it's not as easy to bounce it and have it land atop a stack. Truly, this is a hard trick to perform consistently.

Getting Started

You'll need 6 chips for this trick.

Step One. Stack up 5 chips, alternating colors, and hold 1 chip edgewise between your thumb and middle finger. As with a number of the tricks described in this book, choosing an appropriate surface is important. This trick works nicely on a mouse pad, a hard surface that has a little give.

Step Two. Drop or strike (depending on the surface) the chip between your fingers such that it hits the surface and pops up landing on top of the stack of chips. When dropping the chip you'll need to angle it slightly toward the stack; this will ensure that it bounces in that direction.

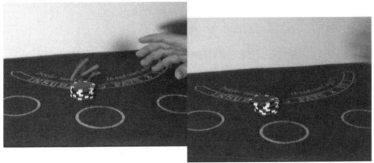

Before You Move On

Pay close attention to height and angle at which you're dropping the chip. Performing this trick with consistent success will
depend upon near exact duplication of the chip drop.

Just for Fun

Try bouncing a chip on top of a stack of 7 chips. Also try this
trick out on different surfaces. You'll discover that different surfaces will require the chip drop be done at different heights and
angles.

THE CHIP BACKSPIN

This is probably one of the easiest tricks to learn, yet one of the
most impressive to watch.

Getting Started

This trick requires only 1 chip.

This trick can be done on any surface; however, it's easier to
learn this trick on a surface that has a little give to it.

Step One. Firmly hold one chip between your thumb and index
finger at approximately 2 o'clock.

Step Two. With force, strike the bottom edge of the chip against whatever surface you're using. Your fingers need to follow through with the downward motion until they actually touch the surface. This imparts backspin.

Step Three. Watch as the chip spins away from you on its edge and then comes right back.

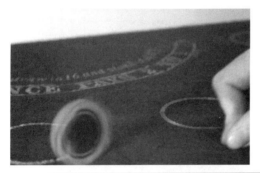

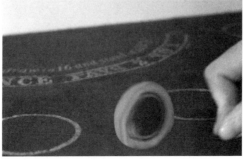

Okay, we'll be honest: when you're first learning this trick, Step Three often doesn't resemble our picture. Horrifyingly, the chip may not even be moving away from you when you strike it. Don't worry. First, check your grip position. It is very important that you grip the chip at 2 o'clock. Holding it too high or too low is not conducive to imparting backspin. If you already are holding it at 2 o'clock, but it's still not working, try tightening your grip. You just may not be holding the chip firmly enough to impart the backspin. If one of those fixes doesn't work, try adjusting the force with which you're striking the chip.

Another problem that people run into with this step is that the chip rolls off to one side or the other as it spins away or comes back. That problem is much more easily fixed; you simply need to concentrate on keeping the chip completely vertical when you're striking it against the table.

Step Four. Catch the chip between your thumb and index finger when it returns.

Before You Move On

You need to be extremely consistent with this trick before you can use it during an actual game. Make sure you can do this at least five times in a row without any problems before you consider yourself a master.

And if you haven't been practicing this on an actual poker table, please note that the strength with which you strike the chip will probably need to be adjusted. Keep this in mind when you move from your practice surface to a felt table.

Just for Fun

Check your accuracy by doing the Chip Backspin between two stacks—goalposts, if you will.

THE CHIP ROLL

Here's a trick you've probably seen before. It's a fun trick though not recommended for the poker table unless you're confident both that you can pull it off and you've got a lot of room to work with (i.e., heads up at the final table).

Getting Started

Grab 3 chips of any color. You can go for more than 3 chips if you want, but the level of difficulty increases with each chip you add.

This trick can be done on any surface, though the harder and smoother the surface the more difficult it is to complete. A table covered by a tablecloth works nicely. If you want to practice at the office, make sure to grab a legal pad when heading to a meeting; it's the perfect surface and just the right amount of space once you get good.

Step One. Hold the chips between your thumb and index finger, with your hand angled toward 2 o'clock. The other hand, the catching hand, should be angled toward 2 o'clock as well. The larger the gap between the hands the more difficult the trick becomes. We suggest starting with your hands no more than twelve inches apart.

Step Two. Release the outermost chip from your hand by ever so slightly lifting your thumb. Only the outermost chip should be released by this maneuver. If more than one chip is released, you don't have enough control over this aspect of the trick, and you'll need to keep practicing.

Step Three. The released chip is caught by the catching hand, which should be angled in such a way that the chip lodges under it and stays upright. If the chip goes underneath the catching hand yet doesn't stay upright, you'll probably need to re-angle the catching hand closer to the table surface. You may need to play around with the angle of the catching hand a bit before you get it right.

Step Four. Steps Two and Three should be repeated for each of the remaining chips. The chips should be lodging in next to each other.

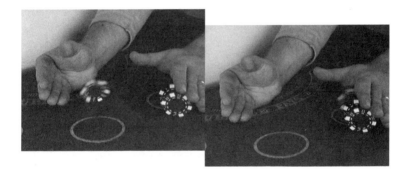

Before You Move On

Make sure you catch your chips in consecutive order. If your third chip lodges between the first two chips, you'll need to keep practicing. Concentrate on the timing of your chip release as well. This trick looks best when each chip release occurs simultaneously with the previous chip being caught.

Just for Fun

If the Chip Roll is a snap for you with 3 chips try it with 4 or 5 chips. See what the maximum number that you can successfully roll is.

THE 4-CHIP CUT

This is a really neat trick and, if you know how to do the Front-to-Back Switch (pp. 29–35) and/or Thumb Roll (pp. 21–25), it shouldn't be too hard to learn.

Getting Started

At the risk of stating the obvious, you need 4 chips for the 4-Chip Cut. For best effect, use 2 chips of one color and 2 of another.

Step One. Place the 4 chips in your hand as if you're doing the Thumb Roll. The 2 outside chips should be one color; the 2 inside chips should be another color.

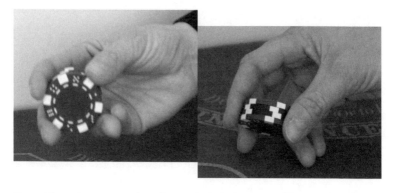

Step Two. Use your thumb to slightly loosen the inner and then the outer chip. This will make the next step easier.

Step Three. Roll the inner and outer chips up your index finger. It's just like the Thumb Roll (and good practice for the Twirl)!

Step Four. Roll the chips back down, but with the outer chip cutting between the two middle chips.

If you can't seem to get the outer chip between the middle chips, you may need to use your middle finger to angle the middle chips slightly away from your palm. To accomplish this, just pull your middle finger back (toward your palm) until the outer chip is positioned properly above the 2 middle chips.

Step Five. Make sure everyone can see the new color pattern of your chips!

Before You Move On

Be sure you can do this without the new outer chip falling out of your hand. If this is happening, simply use the tip of your middle finger to hold it in place during the cut.

Just for Fun

Do a Thumb Roll and then go straight into the 4-Chip Cut. This will eliminate the need to loosen the chips and makes for a very smooth-looking combination!

THE CHIP SLIDE

Here's a trick that's fun and flashy, though better suited to a carnival than a card room.

Getting Started

Grab 3 chips, 2 of one color and 1 of another.

Step One. Hold the 3 chips between your ring and index fingers, using your middle finger to provide support. The odd-color chip should be in the middle of the stack.

Step Two. Roll the inner chip onto your pinky with your thumb, and hold this chip firmly, edgewise, between your pinky and thumb.

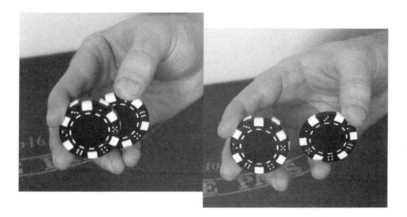

Step Three. Align the edge of the chip between your thumb and pinky with the edge of the inner chip between your ring and index fingers. This is the most difficult and important part of the trick—the alignment means everything. Until you've mastered this trick, take this part very slowly. Focus on the alignment of the chips: they should be lined up and perfectly straight. Any tilt at all may prove disastrous later on, so, again, go slow here. If you try to do this quickly, you will probably blow the alignment.

Step Four. Now you're ready for the slide move! If your hand isn't already in position, you'll need to move it into the slide position (middle finger at the top, thumb at the bottom). This moves the two chips between your ring and index fingers into enough of a vertical position to allow gravity to do its thing. You'll see the outer of the top two chips will eventually slide down and rest between your pinky and thumb. The sliding chip will need to be caught snugly between your thumb and pinky when it gets down there.

You may find that the chip that needs to slide sometimes doesn't cooperate and do so smoothly. It may stick to the other chip and refuse to slide or it may just plummet down uncontrollably. Some chips are inherently slicker than others; newer chips will almost always be slicker than older chips. So besides the basic foolishness of this trick, this lack of reliability is another reason why this trick is definitely not recommended for the poker table. It really can go horribly wrong.

Step Five. After the slide occurs, position the chip between your ring and index finger, behind that of the two chips between your thumb and pinky. It's often helpful to use your middle finger as support behind the chip when making this move.

Before You Move On

Make sure you've got the slide move down because we're going to move on to a variation of this carnival trick that uses the slide move over and over.

Just for Fun

See how many times in a row you can do the Chip Slide.

THE SALT SHAKER

After mastering the Chip Slide you should be able to transition pretty easily into this trick.

Steps One through Four of this trick are identical to that of the Chip Slide; refer back to pages 83–87 for those steps.

Step Five. Rotate your hand counterclockwise moving from 12:00 o'clock to 6:00 o'clock, then clockwise from 6:00 o'clock to 12:00 o'clock, and repeat to your heart's content. This movement will continuously slide the chip back and forth. In order to help ensure that you don't lose control of the sliding chip, you'll want to slightly angle the static chips backward. If you hold these chips perfectly vertical, it becomes much more likely that you'll lose control of the sliding chip.

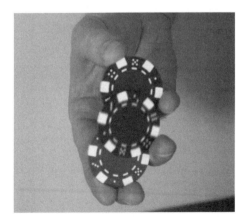

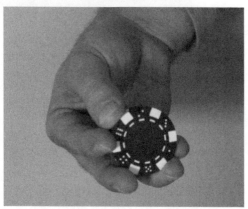

Before You Move On

Take note of the true novelty in this trick. As with the Chip Back-spin and Chip Roll, there is a chip in this trick, the sliding chip, that loses contact with your fingers. While the loss of contact with fingers isn't as dramatic here as in the other two tricks, it has a similar air of complexity for the observer without being as difficult to perform.

Just for Fun

To give this trick some variety, switch between the Chip Slide and the Salt Shaker. Do each of these tricks a couple times before switching to the other.

THE PULL-UNDER

This is the harder cousin of the Pull-Up! It looks deceptively easy but actually requires a lot of practice.

Getting Started

You can do this trick with as few as 2 chips, but we think it works best with 4.

Step One. Grip the chips slightly above their midpoint, using just your thumb and middle fingers. The chips sit on your middle finger just below the top knuckle. The index finger also touches the chips for stability.

Step Two. Use your ring finger to reach around to the front and pull the outermost chip down and underneath the rest of the chips.

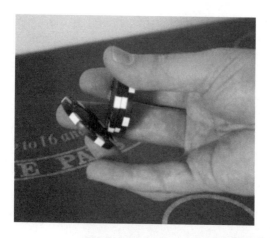

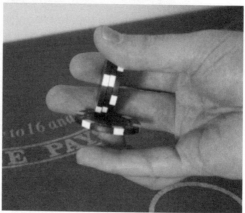

Step Three. The chip you pulled under will start to stand straight up when you have it on the inside. At this point, use your pinky to push it into place. It is now the innermost chip of the stack.

Before You Move On

It's important that the chips stand straight up during the Pull-Under. If you are having trouble with chips tilting during the trick, use your index finger for added stability.

Just for Fun

Alternate the Pull-Up with the Pull-Under.

It's Magic

Even though you now know tons of tricks and are practically a chip trick expert, the tricks in this section won't come easily. They are the hardest of the hard. You will get frustrated trying to learn them. You will want to throw chips . . . storm around . . . scream. . .

Just keep at it. Mastery will come and with it a gigantic sense of accomplishment. Huge. The first time you do the Butterfly, you'll grin for hours.

Anyway, this section starts off with the Twirls. They're the easiest of the hard. Then we tackle the Knuckle Rolls, and then . . . the Butterfly. Are you ready?

THE TWIRLS

Classic Twirl

This is the most common twirl. It looks best when done fast, so practice hard!

Getting started. You need 3 chips.

Step One. This trick starts in the same chip position as the Thumb Roll, same grip tension too.

Step Two. If you need to, use your thumb to slightly loosen the inner and outer chips, then roll the inner and outer chips up your index finger. It's just like the Thumb Roll! At the same time, roll the middle chip down. If you have a large hand, you may only need to roll the chip down to your ring finger.

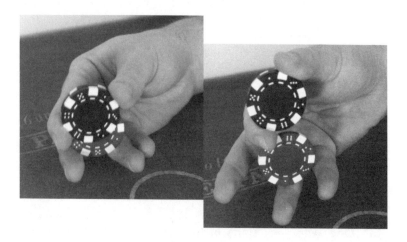

If your hand is smaller, you may need to roll the middle chip all the way down to your pinky to achieve enough room to twirl the chip.

Here's what that looks like.

Step Three. Remember the Spin? Now's the time to use it! Put your middle finger on the outside edge of the chip, and use it to spin the chip clockwise 180 degrees by pulling it back toward the palm of your hand.

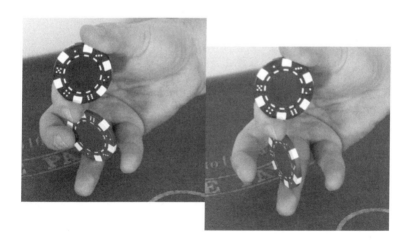

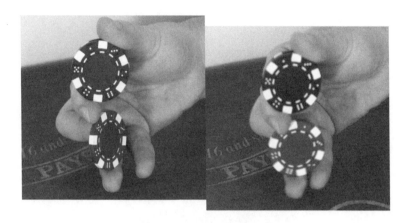

Step Four. Roll the inner and outer chips back down while pushing the middle chip back up. This puts you back in original position and ready to twirl again.

Before you move on. As we suggested in the Just for Fun section of the 4-Chip Cut, if you're having a problem separating the inner and outer chips from the middle chip, do a Thumb Roll and then go straight into the trick. This will eliminate the need to loosen the chips, and it looks good too!

Just for fun. See if you can twirl the chip 360, 540, or even 720 degrees before moving it back up into position.

Front Twirl

This is a variation on the Classic Twirl. Some think it actually looks sharper than the Classic Twirl because the spinning is right out in front for all to see. You be the judge.

Getting started. This is a 3-chip trick.

Step One. Stand the chips straight up between your ring finger and pinky. Your middle and index fingers may also touch the chips for stability.

Step Two. Hold the inner chip steady with your thumb and the outer chip firmly with your index finger, then tilt your hand down until the middle chip falls out.

Step Three. Transfer the grip of the outer chip from the index finger to the thumb. Your index finger is now free to grip the top edge of the inner chip. Now extend your index and ring fingers away from the other chips; the front chip needs to be far enough away so that you can spin freely.

Step Four. Put your middle finger on the front edge of the chip, and use it to spin the chip clockwise 180 degrees by pulling it back toward the palm of your hand. This is the same move as the Spin but performed in a different hand location.

Step Five. After the spin, again place your middle finger on the front edge of the chip, and use it to push the chip back into place.

Before you move on. Spend extra time on Step Two. It is a move unlike any other that has been taught in this book and will take extra time to master. At first, it will and should feel unfamiliar and unnatural, but, with practice, you will soon catch on.

Just for fun. Instead of putting the chip back in the middle after the spin, try placing it on the far right. It looks neat, and you can mix it up with the traditional front twirl for some variety.

THE KNUCKLE ROLLS

Have you ever had a time when you were really sick or in a lot of pain, and when you told the story later on, you remember that it hurt and you remember your reactions to it, but you don't really remember what the actual pain felt like? That's kind of what it's like for us to talk about learning the Knuckle Rolls.

We've read of people who claim they learned the Knuckle Rolls in 15 minutes, and to them we say, "LIAR!" Just kidding. We're sure it's possible, but these were really killers for us to learn. The motion is unlike any other covered in this book, and we recommend that you mentally prepare yourself for a battle; the Forward Knuckle Roll is going to take a while to learn, and you're going to drop a lot of chips along the way. Remember, no pain, no gain!

Forward Knuckle Roll

You must learn the Knuckle Roll in the forward or thumb-to-pinky direction before learning the backward or pinky-to-thumb version.

Getting started. This is a 1-chip trick.

Step One. Hold the chip loosely between your thumb and index finger, in a semi-vertical or vertical position.

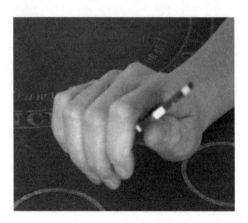

Step Two. Lift your thumb up and to the left. If you do this slowly, it will carefully release the chip until it rests atop your index finger. At the same time, create space by moving your middle finger up and as far to the right as it will go. This is an exaggeration of the motion. As time goes by, you will know exactly how much space you really need to create, but for learning purposes, it is best to create as large a gap as possible.

Step Three. Keep your middle finger raised, but move it slowly back toward the chip. When it touches the chip, move your middle finger down. This motion should stand the chip straight up.

Step Four. Release the chip by moving your index finger slowly up and to the left. The chip should now rest atop your middle finger. At the same time, create space by moving your ring finger up and as far to the right as it will go.

Step Five. Keep your ring finger raised, but move it slowly back toward the chip. When it touches the chip, move your ring finger down. This motion should stand the chip straight up.

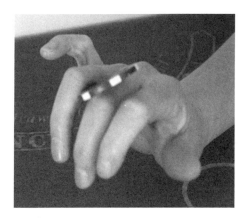

Step Six. Release the chip by moving your middle finger slowly up and to the left. The chip should now rest atop your ring finger. At the same time, create space by moving your pinky finger up and as far to the right as it will go.

Step Seven. Keep your pinky raised, but move it slowly back toward the chip. When it touches the chip, move your pinky down. This motion should stand the chip straight up.

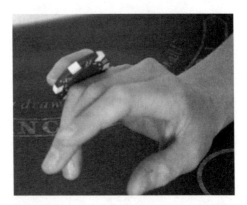

Step Eight. Slowly slide your ring finger up the chip, being careful to keep enough pressure between your ring finger and the chip and the chip and the pinky to ensure that the chip doesn't drop. The middle and index fingers should copy the motion of the ring finger. As you do this, the chip will start to angle in toward the palm of your hand. At the same time bring your thumb across the palm of your hand, and place it on the face of the chip.

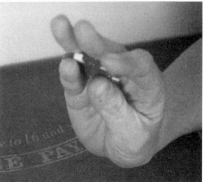

Step Nine. Slide the chip across the underside of your fingers and back to the starting position.

Before you move on. If you find that you are able to get the chip all the way across your knuckles, but are then losing it off the edge of your hand, try this: using your other hand, simply place the chip straight up between your ring finger and pinky, then practice Step Eight over and over.

Just for fun. Try to do the Knuckle Roll with both hands simultaneously!

Backward Knuckle Roll

After you've mastered the Forward Knuckle Roll, you'll want to know how to reverse it. It's only natural. The good news is that the Backward Knuckle Roll is easier to learn than the Forward Knuckle Roll. The bad news is . . . it's still not easy!

Getting started. This is a 1-chip trick.

Step One. This trick begins at Step Seven of the Forward Knuckle Roll; the chip is standing straight up between the ring finger and the pinky.

Step Two. Move your pinky up and to the right; this will release the chip and result in the chip resting atop your ring finger. At the same time, create space by moving your middle finger up and as far to the left as it will go.

If you're having trouble getting the chip to fall to the left, try angling your hand; your thumb should be significantly lower than your pinky.

Step Three. Keep your middle finger raised, but move it slowly back toward the chip. When it touches the chip, move your middle finger down. This motion should stand the chip straight up.

Step Four. Release the chip by moving your ring finger slowly up and to the right. The chip should now rest atop your middle finger. At the same time, create space by moving your index finger up and as far to the left as it will go.

Step Five. Keep your index finger raised, but move it slowly back toward the chip. When it touches the chip, move your index finger down. This motion should stand the chip straight up.

Step Six. Release the chip by moving your middle finger slowly up and to the right. The chip should now rest atop your index finger.

Step Seven. Grab the edge of the chip with your thumb, and stand the chip straight up between your thumb and index finger. The Backward Knuckle Roll is now complete. This is the starting position for the Forward Knuckle Roll.

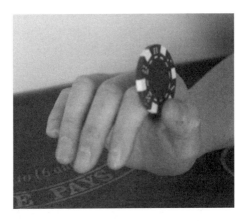

Before you move on. Make sure you can do the backward version as fast as you can do the forward one.

Just for fun. See how many times you can do the Forward and Backward Knuckle Rolls without dropping the chip. If you can do it at least three times, you'll know you have the Knuckle Rolls mastered.

THE BUTTERFLY

Okay, are you ready? Have you learned most of the other tricks in this book? Well then, let's get started with the trick that many believe to be the most difficult of all. If you learn this trick you can consider yourself a master of chip tricks—like us.

Getting Started

You'll need 4 chips for this trick. Again, stack the chips in alternating color to provide a little contrast and a little extra flash—though this trick leaves mouths open wide even without the added color contrast.

Step One. Hold the stack of 4 chips midway between your index and ring fingers. If needed, you can touch the chips with your middle finger to help stabilize them.

Step Two. Using your thumb, roll the bottom 2 chips up your index finger.

Step Three. Using your index finger, roll the top 2 chips across your ring finger, wedging these chips between your ring finger and pinky.

Step Four. Move your index finger off of and away from the chips between your ring finger and pinky. Slide your middle finger between the two stacks of chips.

Step Five. At this point, ensure that the back of your middle finger is touching the chip between your ring finger and pinky and the chip between your thumb and index finger.

Step Six. For the majority, this is the most difficult step. We're going to fan the chips out across our fingers. The middle finger should hold the chips touching it stable; as the thumb rolls outward the chip between it and the index finger (the bottom chip)

and the pinky rolls outward the chip between it and the ring finger (the top chip). Stretch your thumb and pinky out as far as you can.

Step Seven. Now it's time to bring the chips back together to form one stack. You're pretty much going to do what you've done previously, but now in reverse. Roll the outer two chips back upon the inner two chips. Move the two stacks of chips outward, creating enough space for the middle finger to move outward through the stacks. Then move the 2 chips between your ring finger and pinky on top of the 2 chips between your thumb and index finger. Again, the motions for moving these chips back together should be the reverse of the motions you used to fan the chips out.

Before You Move On

For those of us with smallish hands, fanning the chip between the ring finger and pinky can present some problems. One that typically occurs with this move is that the chip falls out from between these two fingers prior to full extension. Do your best to keep this chip from riding up the ring finger; the more horizontal you keep this chip while you're rolling it outward the greater the likelihood you'll be able to fully fan it out.

Just for Fun

Those with sizable hands can use 8 chips for this trick, fanning out 2 chips between each pair of fingers.

For an additional wow, learn to do this with your left (or non-dominant) hand, and do the Butterfly with both hands simultaneously. If you can do this, congratulations, you've graduated at the top of the class!

Killer Combos

Each of the many tricks you have now mastered is impressive and unique, but—there's no denying it—they look infinitely better done in combination. We're not recommending that you work up a routine and dance around to music while performing your tricks, but we do suggest that you have a couple of killer combos in your repertoire.

Below we list some 2-, 3-, and 4-trick combos that we like, but remember, you know a lot of tricks, so be sure to work out some additional combos on your own!

2-Trick Combos

- Thumb Roll + Vertical Back-to-Front Switch
- Pull-Up + Pull-Under

3-Trick Combos

- Finger Chip Flip + Horizontal Back-to-Front Switch + Horizontal Flip Switch

4-Trick Combos

- Thumb Roll + Classic Twirl + Finger Chip Flip + Front Twirl

Again, if you can't do these, or if you don't find these combos impressive enough, then make up some of your own. The key to coming up with good combos is the ease of transition from one trick to another. Keep the finger positioning in mind when you're creating the combo; combos look best when the completed finger positioning of the first trick is the starting finger positioning of the second trick—and so on for successive tricks. Good luck!

Safety First

Now that you know all the tricks, common sense should tell you that not all of them are appropriate to perform at the poker table. Some are just too dangerous: too easy to mess up and consequently likely to make you look like a chump. You *should* know that, but you may not, so we rate the tricks below. Here's the scale that we use. We call it the Table-Friendly Scale (TFS):

1 = This trick is totally safe to use at the table. Even if you mess up, you won't hurt anyone or your table cred.

2 = There's a level of risk associated with this trick, but if you do pull it off, you'll look like a god. Go for it if you're good!

3 = Are you crazy?! You could put out someone's eye!

* = This trick is just too weird to do at the table. Do you want people to think you're a freak?

The Thumb Roll	1
The Finger Chip Flip	1
The Switches (All)	1
The Pull-Up	1
The Somersault	1
The Chip Snaps (Top and Bottom)	1*
The Shuffle	1
The Bottom Chip Flip	1
The Chip Sweep	3
The Bounce	3
The Chip Backspin	2
The Chip Roll	2*
The 4-Chip Cut	1
The Chip Slide	2*
The Pull-Under	1
The Twirls (Classic and Front)	2
The Knuckle Rolls (Forward and Backward)	2
The Butterfly	3*

Table Smartz

(Don't Look Like Dead Money)

Okay, so now you're fully armed with tricks, and you've just learned which tricks are safe to take to the table. Can you use them to your advantage at the poker table?

Although there are definitely certain circumstances in which you can use chip tricks to your advantage at the poker table, truth be told, they won't help you when you're playing against your friends. In a home game, with players you know well and who know you well, chip tricks will do little more than provide a bit of entertainment and perhaps encourage the group to make a few more jokes at your expense. (Though it's our hope that your friends will be so impressed and dazzled by your finger feats that they will want to learn them too, we realize that that's a long shot.) Don't expect chip tricks to earn you respect among friends because your friends already know what type of poker player you are; a well-executed shuffle isn't going to change their opinion.

Also, if you have little to no skill, you can't expect chip tricks to work too well for you either. Truly, they may spare you the moniker "dead money" for a round or two, but it's inevitable that you will be unmasked for the true newbie you are. Remember, chip tricks can't perform miracles!

When will they work, you wonder? Here's when: if you're at least a low-level intermediate player and you're playing against people who don't know you, especially newer players, such as those you might meet at a casino, then you may be able to use your tricks to gain a slight advantage over them.

Here are some do's:

- Do use chip tricks when you first sit down at a table. This will signify to others at the table that you're no newbie, which may help to give you more credibility than you deserve. Keep in mind that this advantage may only last for a very short time; the way you play your cards will soon be the most significant factor as to whether or not you deserve respect.

- Do use them when you want to intimidate an opponent. A large raise in conjunction with an impressive chip trick such as the Twirl may be just enough to get that opponent on the fence to fold.

- Do use chip tricks to help yourself calm down. We've all had those nervous, shaky moments at the table. The repetitive movement of a chip trick is sure to stabilize those nerves.

- Do use chip tricks to disguise your glee. For example, a player just bet into your royal flush on the turn. You're so excited. You want to bet immediately, but you know it's better to look like you're considering your options before making your play. Use a chip trick or two to kill some time before betting.

And some definite don'ts:

- Don't allow your chip tricks to become a tell. If you consistently use chip tricks in the same situation, such as when you're bluffing, others will surely catch on to this. Be aware of what you're doing; don't allow your chip tricks to become detrimental to your game.

- Don't overuse chip tricks. The other players will soon become immune to them if you're doing tricks nonstop at the table. In fact, you may actually become a target if your tricks are annoying others; the incessant chatter of chips has been known to set some people off.

- Don't do tricks that you haven't mastered. This is critical and should be obvious, but we have to say it. You will look like a chump if the chip you're knuckle rolling falls off your hand and lands in someone else's stack.

Bottom line, chip tricks can give you an edge if incorporated into your game intelligently. Remember, though, it's a very small edge and it decreases over time, meaning the longer you sit at a table, the less impact your chip tricks will have. Ultimately, your play will determine your fate. But if you ever find someone who's truly awed by your shuffle, who folds at the site of your Twirl and nervously giggles when they see your Knuckle Roll, well . . . you need to stay at that table and take all their money!

What's Next?

If you've learned all the tricks in this book, congratulations! That's quite a feat, and you should be very proud of yourself. Your chip trick career should not end here, though (unless you want it to). Continue learning. Continue growing. Use your imagination and know-how to create new variations on old tricks—or just plain old new tricks. And be sure to share your knowledge and spread the chip trick fever!

Now go LOOK LIKE A POKER PRO!

Finger Stiffness and Flexibility

Odds are that you've probably discovered a few things about chip tricks if you've been practicing enough: (1) there are a few tricks—maybe more then a few—that just don't seem possible because your fingers aren't flexible enough. And (2) after a lot of practice, especially with tricks that involve a lot of knuckle work and/or tendon stretching, your fingers are going to be stiff. The following are a few finger exercises that may help ease the stiffness and may even improve finger flexibility.

These exercises are not intended for treatment of injured hands or fingers. Consult a physician if you're feeling finger discomfort beyond that of stiffness or if stiffness lasts for more than a few days after taking a hiatus from chip tricks.

All stretching should be slow and gradual, to the point of feeling tension, not pain.

1. Using the eraser end of a pencil for support, bend the end joint of your finger, keeping the other joints on that finger straight and then straighten out the end joint. Repeat this five times with each finger.

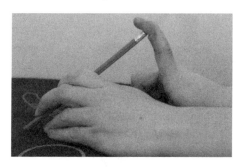

2. Bend all your finger joints while keeping your knuckles straight, and touch the top of your palm, hold for five seconds. Repeat this five times.

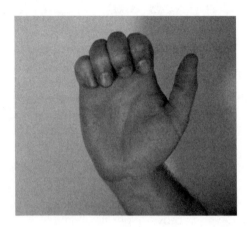

3. Using your thumb, reach across your palm to the base of your pinky while keeping the fingers straight; hold for five seconds. Repeat this five times.

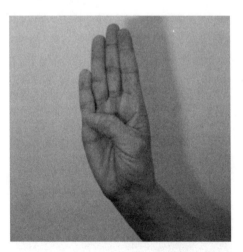

4. While laying your palm down on a flat surface, extend all fingers outward, taking special care to keep all parts of your hand touching the surface; hold for five seconds, then bring your fingers together again. Repeat this five times.

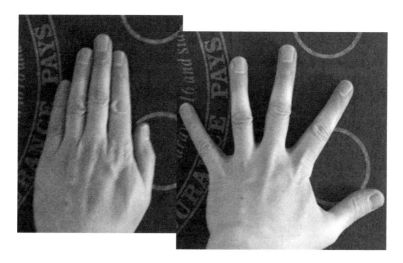

5. With the right hand outstretched in front of you, gently pull the index finger back until you feel the stretch, hold for five seconds, and repeat three times. This exercise should be targeted at stiff fingers and/or fingers that need increased flexibility.

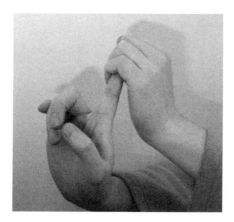

6. With the base of your palm on a flat surface, curl your finger around a tennis ball or similar size round object. Make sure to stretch your finger as far as you can during this exercise. Hold for three seconds, and repeat three times with each finger.

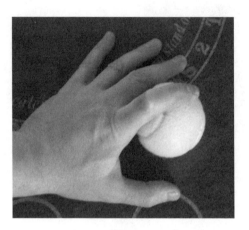

7. Push a poker chip down between fingers to the point of tension, not pain. Hold for three seconds. Repeat between all pairs of fingers three times.

The Lowdown on Poker Chips

We're going to keep this brief. There are lots of different chips, and you can do chip tricks with any of them—even the cheap plastic ones you buy at the corner drugstore. Not all chips are created equal, however.

The chips that you see us using in this book are 11.5 gram clay composites. Nice chips. We recommend them. They're great to learn tricks with because they have a little heft. You learn to really feel what the chips are doing, and you won't have any problems transitioning your way down to a lighter chip later. The one complaint we have about them is that they're a little slippery.

God knows, you won't have that problem with a casino chip. Casino chips are usually a little lighter (8.5 grams) and have—um, a texture. Part of that texture is intentional and part is, well, dirt. This makes them good for doing the Shuffle but really bad for doing something like the Chip Slide.

Again, our advice is to take some time and get acquainted with whatever chips you are using before trying any tricks. It's the low-risk move, and at the table, when money's involved, that's also the smart move.